MALCOLM ARCHER

INTRADA

MUSIC DEPARTMENT

OXFORD
UNIVERSITY PRESS

for TJS

Intrada

MALCOLM ARCHER

Sw.: **Full without 16'**
Gt.: **8', 4', 2', Mixture, Sw. to Gt.**
Ped.: **16', 8', Reed 16', Gt. to Ped., Sw. to Ped.**

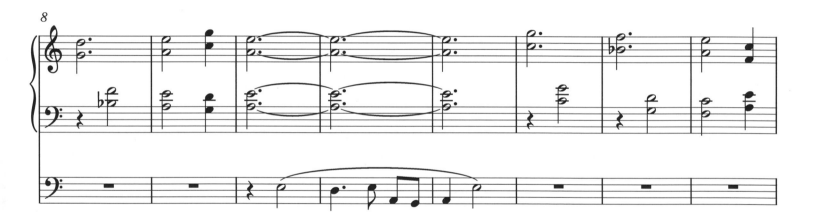

Printed in Great Britain

OXFORD UNIVERSITY PRESS, MUSIC DEPARTMENT, GREAT CLARENDON STREET, OXFORD OX2 6DP

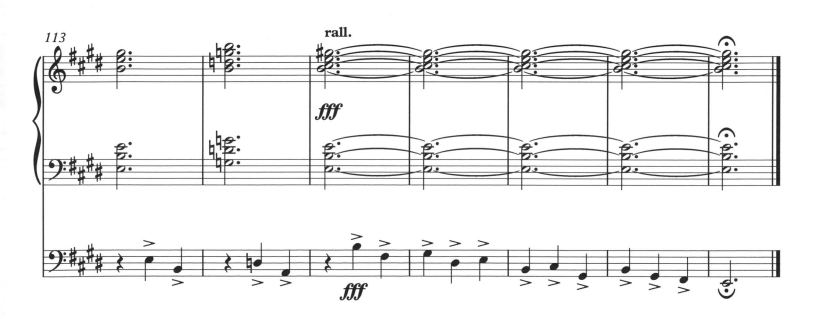